—J.P. MARTIN—

THE
BOOK
OF
AFRICAN
PROVERBS
AND
WISDOM

VOLUME 1
A Collection Of Ancient Proverbs and Wisdom
From The Continent Of Africa

Order this book online at www.trafford.com
or email orders@trafford.com

Most Trafford titles are also available at major online book retailers.

 www.trafford.com

North America & international
toll-free: 844 688 6899 (USA & Canada)
fax: 812 355 4082

Our mission is to efficiently provide the world's finest, most comprehensive book publishing
service, enabling every author to experience success. To find out how to publish your book,
your way, and have it available worldwide, visit us online at www.trafford.com

ISBN: 978-1-6987-1146-1 (sc)

ISBN: 978-1-6987-1145-4 (e)

Print information available on the last page.

Trafford rev. 05/21/2022

ACKNOWLEDGEMENTS

This book is dedicated to my creator to whom I am eternally grateful. This book is also dedicated to all of my family.

By J.P.Martin

INTRODUCTION

The Book of African Proverbs and Wisdom is a collection of over 100 proverbs, inspirational quotes, knowledge, and words of wisdom. The continent of Africa is an extremely culturally rich region and home to over 2,000 languages, 3,000 ethnic groups, numerous belief systems and is also the birthplace of human civilization on planet Earth. A proverb is a simple and insightful, traditional saying that expresses a perceived truth based on common sense or experience. Proverbs are popularly defined as short expressions of popular wisdom. These proverbs have been passed down through the generations and are still widely used all over Africa today. The Book of African Proverbs and Wisdom provides an abundance of knowledge and wisdom that can be utilized within your life to benefit yourself and your loved ones.

Instruction in youth is like engraving in stones

North African Proverb

When the cow falls;
many knives appear

Tunisian Proverb

Love is like a baby, it needs
to be treated tenderly

Congolese Proverb

A good woman
should be as bright
as sunshine, as
black as ink, and as
sweet as honey

Ghanaian Proverb

Justice is like fire, even if you cover it with a veil, it still burns

Madagascan Proverb

You may feed an ungrateful man for a whole year, but in return he may not offer you a single dinner

Tunisian Proverb

It is better to be loved
than feared

Sierra Leonean Proverb

Do not set pen on papyrus
to cheat a man for it
is hateful to God,
Do not bear false witness
with lying words, nor lend
your tongue to support
the perjury of another

Ancient Egyptian Proverb

Only the patient person will win the daughter of the Hausa man

Hausa Proverb

He who falls victim to his enemies can expect no mercy

Ghanaian Proverb

Wisdom is wealth

Swahili Proverb

When herdsmen squabble,
the camels do not drink

Somali Proverb

He who wants to cross a river
must not be afraid of getting wet

Zambian Proverb

The eye will not agree not to
discover the beautiful one;
It is hard for the heart
to relinquish love.
The heart has no brain,
the eye has no curtain.
Refrain.
Blame both of them, do
not blame just one.

Swahili Proverb

When a man is stung he does not destroy all beehives

Hausa Proverb

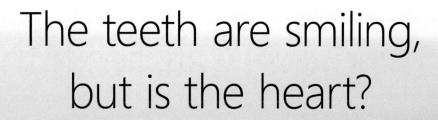

The teeth are smiling,
but is the heart?

Congolese Proverb

Nothing ever satisfies a thief

Yoruba Proverb

Your friends and relations always want a share of your goods

Hausa Proverb

A woman without a
good husband is like a
field without a seed

Ethiopian Proverb

Once you have been tossed
by a buffalo, a black ox
looks like a buffalo

Kenyan Proverb

A beautiful finger will get a ring put around it

Swahili Proverb

Gossips always suspect that others are talking about them

Nigerian Proverb

A good name is more valuable
than a velvet garment

Moroccan Proverb

Cowards have no scars

Zimbabwean Proverb

Anger is the father
of hopelessness

Yoruba Proverb

Giving alms never
lessens the purse

West African Proverb

Whoever is in a hurry to enjoy life will go to heaven in a hurry

Yoruba Proverb

Hasty marriages bring
hasty divorces

Ethiopian Proverb

Reading books removes
sorrows from the heart

Moroccan Proverb

Whoever does not respect
you, insults you

Moroccan Proverb

When the leg does not work the stomach does not eat

Congolese Proverb

No lamb has ever been
born with it's wool on

Moroccan Proverb

Profit is profit, even in Mecca

Hausa Proverb

Do not boast of your knowledge, but seek the advice of the untutored as much as the well educated

The Instructions of Ptahhotep, Ancient Egypt

Work on your reputation until it is established, when it is established it will work for you

Tunisian Proverb

It is foolish to start a fire
just to see the flames

Ethiopian Proverb

Abundance of wealth
is a trial for man

Moroccan Proverb

A secret for two, is soon
a secret for nobody

Algerian Proverb

A hyena cannot smell
it's own stench

Namibian Proverb

Gifts are the key to
the female heart

Zimbabwean Proverb

No matter how long the night
the dawn will surely break

Hausa Proverb

55

A ripened fruit does not cling to the vine

Zimbabwean Proverb

A prudent man who knows proverbs, resolves problems

Botswanian Proverb

A fool at age forty,
is a fool indeed

Ethiopian Proverb

No matter how much the world changes, cats will never lay eggs

Kenyan Proverb

He who waits for a chance
may wait a long time

Nigerian Proverb

God is our general
in a time of war

Botswanian Proverb

The ways of the immoral
are always predictable

Namibian Proverb

Once we have something
we take it for granted

Algerian Proverb

The fool speaks often but
the wise man listens

Gabonese Proverb

If a bird does not fly, it goes to bed hungry

Akan Proverb (Ghana)

Do not blame God for creating the tiger, just thank him for not giving it wings

Ethiopian Proverb

It is not only one road that leads to the market

Yoruba Proverb

A fool thinks he is being praised
while he is being insulted

Ethiopian Proverb

The body is easily satisfied
but not the heart

Angolan Proverb

72

Knowledge is like a field, if it is neither plowed nor guarded it will not be harvested

Fulani Proverb

Do not catch a leopard by it's tail, but if you do then do not let it go

Ethiopian Proverb

Beautiful words don't put
porridge in the pot

Botswanian Proverb

A king's child is a servant
in foreign lands

Zimbabwean Proverb

Order is the first law of heaven

Yoruba Proverb

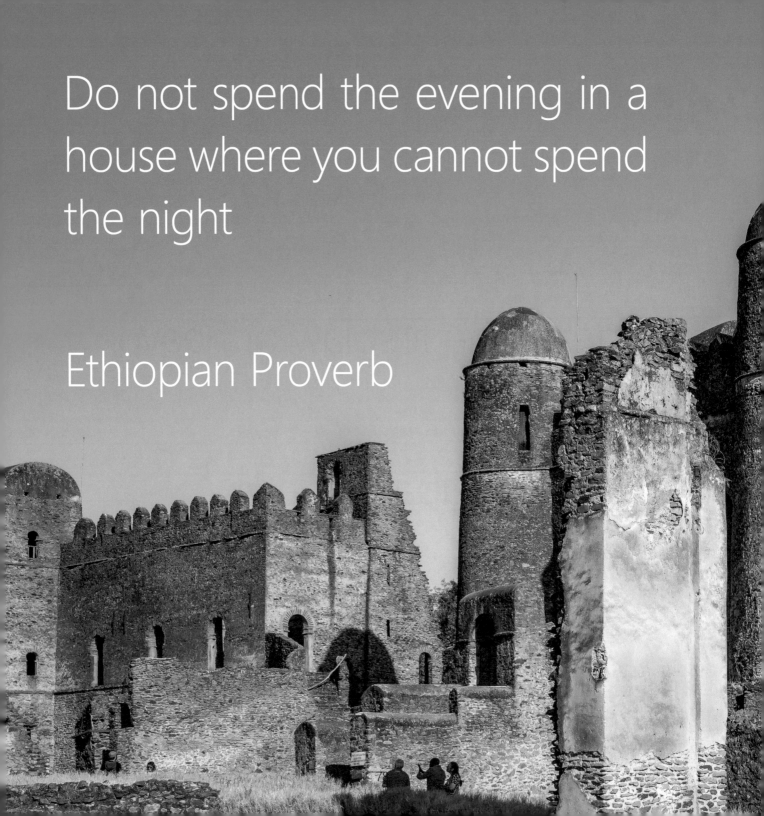

Do not spend the evening in a house where you cannot spend the night

Ethiopian Proverb

A diamond's father is coal, yet it regards itself as upper-class

Namibian Proverb

What comes easily goes easily

Akan Proverb (Ghana)

Do not set sail under
someone else's star

Swahili Proverb

Speak kindly or refrain
from talking

Algerian Proverb

A good wife is easy to find,
but suitable in-laws are rare

Madagascan Proverb

To be happy in one's home
is better than to be a chief

Nigerian Proverb

Take a wife while you are young so that she may make a son for you while you are youthful

Nigerian Proverb

Peace is costly, but it is worth the expense

Kenyan Proverb

Water does not stay in the sky forever

Kenyan Proverb

The chameleon looks in all directions before moving

Ugandan Proverb

Marry for love, work for money

Nigerian Proverb

A fool is a wise man's ladder

South African Proverb

It is better to be poor when one is young, rather than becoming poor at old age

Kenyan Proverb

Patience can cook a stone

Fulani Proverb

The cries of a goat do not prevent it from reaching the market

Kenyan Proverb

Instruct a man, you instruct an individual. Instruct a woman, you instruct a nation

Nigerian Proverb

Children are the reward of life

Congolese Proverb

A domesticated dog does
not know how to hunt

Yoruba Proverb

Wells must be dug today to quench the thirst of tomorrow

Fulani Proverb

A woman who is not successful in her own marriage, has no advice for her younger generations

Nigerian Proverb

Distance breeds respect

Nigerian Proverb

Bad friends prevent you
from having good friends

Gabonese Proverb

Lying can get you a wife,
but it won't keep her

Cameroonian Proverb

A man who falls into a well will seize even the edge of a sword

Hausa Proverb

Ask for a camel when you
expect to get a goat

Sudanese Proverb

A man with wealth will
always get a servant

Hausa Proverb

One who is looking for a wife does not speak with contempt about women

Nigerian Proverb

When God wills that an event will occur, he sets the causes that will lead to it

Sudanese Proverb

Be it wickedness or be
it goodness, neither
goes unrequited

Nigerian Proverb

Glaring wildly does not bespeak manliness

Yoruba Proverb

A woman's husband
is her closest kin

Yoruba Proverb

Slowly is the manner in which
termites consume a house

Yoruba Proverb

Silence is also a
form of speech

Fulani Proverb

He who loves a thing
often talks of it

Nigerian Proverb

One who loves
you, warns you

Baganda Proverb

The nuts from a palm tree
don't fall without dragging
a few leaves with it

Congolese Proverb

When the fish gets rotten, it all starts from the head

Namibian Proverb

Little and lasting is better
than much and passing

Moroccan Proverb

He who tells the truth is
not well liked by fools

Bambara Proverb

Bad sand looks for bad clay
(like attracts like)

Nubian Proverb

Seek to perform your duties to your highest abilities, this way your actions will be blameless

Ancient Egyptian Proverb

One falsehood spoils
a thousand truths

Ashanti Proverb

Learn politeness from
the impolite

Egyptian Proverb

Glossary

Printed in the United States
by Baker & Taylor Publisher Services